PISCES

~SUN SIGN SERIES~

GW00730023

PISCES

SUN SIGN SERIES
JOANNA MARTINE WOOLFOLK

TAYLOR TRADE PUBLISHING
LANHAM • NEW YORK • BOULDER • TORONTO • PLYMOUTH, UK

Published by Taylor Trade Publishing
An imprint of The Rowman & Littlefield Publishing Group, Inc.
4501 Forbes Boulevard, Suite 200, Lanham, Maryland 20706
www.rlpgtrade.com

Estover Road, Plymouth PL6 7PY, United Kingdom

Distributed by National Book Network

British Library Cataloguing in Publication Information Available

Library of Congress Cataloging-in-Publication Data

Woolfolk, Joanna Martine.
  Pisces / Joanna Martine Woolfolk.
    p. cm.—(Sun sign series)
  ISBN 978-1-58979-564-8 (pbk. : alk. paper)—ISBN 978-1-58979-539-6 (electronic)
  1. Pisces (Astrology) I. Title.
 BF1727.75.W66 2011
 133.5'277—dc23   2011018436

∞™ The paper used in this publication meets the minimum requirements of American
National Standard for Information Sciences—Permanence of Paper for Printed Library
Materials, ANSI/NISO Z39.48-1992.

Printed in the United States of America

I dedicate this book to the memory of
William Woolfolk
whose wisdom continues to guide me,

and to
James Sgandurra
who made everything bloom again.

CONTENTS

ABOUT THE AUTHOR

Astrologer Joanna Martine Woolfolk has had a long career as an author, columnist, lecturer, and counselor. She has written the monthly horoscope for numerous magazines in the United States, Europe, and Latin America—among them *Marie Claire*, *Harper's Bazaar*, *Redbook*, *Self*, *YM*, *House Beautiful*, and *StarScroll International*. In addition to the best-selling *The Only Astrology Book You'll Ever Need*, Joanna is the author of *Sexual Astrology*, which has sold over a million copies worldwide, and *Astrology Source*, an interactive CD-ROM.

Joanna is a popular television and radio personality who has been interviewed by Barbara Walters, Regis Philbin, and Sally Jessy Raphael. She has appeared in a regular astrology segment on *New York Today* on NBC-TV and on *The Fairfield Exchange* on

CT Cable Channel 12, and she appears frequently on television and radio shows around the country. You can visit her website at www.joannamartinewoolfolk.com.

ACKNOWLEDGMENTS

Many people contribute to the creation of a book, some with ideas and editorial suggestions, and some unknowingly through their caring and love.

Among those who must know how much they helped is Jed Lyons, the elegant, erudite president of my publishers, the Rowman & Littlefield Publishing Group. Jed gave me the idea for this Sun Sign series, and I am grateful for his faith and encouragement.

Enormous gratitude also to Michael K. Dorr, my literary agent and dear friend, who has believed in me since we first met and continues to be my champion. I thank Michael for his sharp editor's eye and imbuing me with confidence.

Two people who don't know how much they give are my beloved sister and brother, Patricia G. Reynhout and Dr. John T. Galdamez. They sustain me with their unfailing devotion and support.

*We are born at a given moment, in a given place,
and like vintage years of wine, we have the
qualities of the year and of the season
in which we are born.*

CARL GUSTAV JUNG

INTRODUCTION

When my publishers suggested I write a book devoted solely to Pisces, I was thrilled. I've long wanted to concentrate exclusively on your wonderful sign. You are very special in the zodiac. Astrology teaches that Pisces is the sign of imagination, fantasy, and intuition. Your sign represents mystery and mysticism, nurturing, sympathy, and deep creativity. The ancients called Pisces the sign of spiritual understanding, for you are in touch with the deeper truths of life. You see into people's emotions and sorrows; in relationships, you merge on a heart level, and your style of loving is selfless. Karmic teachers say you were picked to be Pisces because, in a previous life, you were a mystic and healer who eased the suffering of your fellow man. But whether or not one believes in past lives, in *this* life you are Pisces, the remarkable sign of the artist, creator, and dreamer.

These days it has become fashionable to be a bit dismissive of Sun signs (the sign that the Sun was in at the time of your birth). Some people sniff that "everyone knows about Sun signs." They say the descriptions are too cookie-cutter, too much a cardboard figure, too inclusive (how can every Piscean be the same?).

Of course every Piscean is not the same! And many of these differences not only are genetic and environmental, but are differences in your *charts*. Another Pisces person would not necessarily have your Moon sign, or Venus sign, or Ascendant. However, these are factors to consider later—after you have studied your Sun sign. (In *The Only Astrology Book You'll Ever Need*, I cover in depth differences in charts: different Planets, Houses, Ascendants, etc.)

First and foremost, you are a Piscean. Pisces is the sign the Sun was traveling through at the time of your birth.* The Sun is our most powerful planet. (In astrological terms, the Sun is referred to as a planet even though technically it is a "luminary.") It gives us life, warmth, energy, food. It is the force that sustains us on Earth. The Sun is also the most important and pervasive influence in your horoscope and in many ways determines how others see you. Your Sun sign governs your individuality, your distinctive style, and your drive to fulfill your goals.

Your sign of Pisces symbolizes the role you are given to play in this life. It's as if at the moment of your birth you were pushed onstage into a drama called *This Is My Life*. In this drama, you are the starring actor—and Pisces is the character you play. What aspects of this character are you going to project? The Piscean caring, compassion, sensitivity, and kindness? Its ability to inspire and the magic it brings to people's lives? Or its dependency and weak will, its inclination toward confusion and escapism? Your sign of Pisces describes your journey through this life, for it is your task to evolve into a perfect Piscean.

For each of us, the most interesting, most gripping subject is *self*. The longer I am an astrologer—which at this point is half my

*From our viewpoint here on Earth, the Sun travels around the Earth once each year. Within the space of that year the Sun moves through all twelve signs of the zodiac, spending approximately one month in each sign.

lifetime—the more I realize that what we all want to know about is ourselves. "Who am I?" you ask. You want to know what makes you tick, why you have such intense feelings, and whether others are also insecure. People ask me questions like, "What kind of man should I look for?" "Why am I discontented with my job?" or "The man I'm dating is an Aries; will we be happy together?" They ask me if they'll ever find true love and when they will get out of a period of sadness or fear or the heavy burden of problems. They ask about their path in life and how they can find more fulfillment.

So I continue to see that the reason astrology exists is to answer questions about you. Basically, it's all about *you*. Astrology has been described as a stairway leading into your deeper self. It holds out the promise that you do not have to pass through life reacting blindly to experience, that you can within limits direct your own destiny and in the process reach a truer self-understanding.

Astrologically, the place to begin the study of yourself is your Sun sign. In this book, you'll read about your many positive qualities as well as your Pisces issues and negative inclinations. You'll find insights into your power and potentials, advice about love and sex, career guidance, health and diet tips, and information about myriads of objects, places, concepts, and things to which Pisces is attached. You'll also find topics not usually included in other astrology books—such as how Pisces fits in with Chinese astrology and with numerology.

Come with me on this exploration of the "infinite variety" (in Shakespeare's phrase) of being a Pisces.

Joanna Martine Woolfolk
Stamford, Connecticut
June 2011

PISCES

FEBRUARY 19–MARCH 20

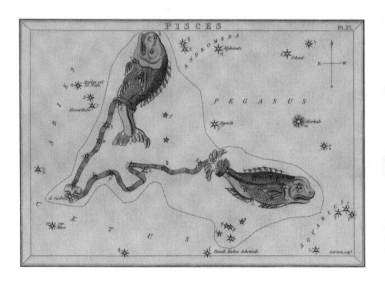

PART ONE

ALL ABOUT YOU

ILLUMINATING QUOTATIONS

"We don't see things as they are. We see them as *we* are."

—Anais Nin, author, a Pisces

"There are two ways to live. You can live as if nothing is a miracle. Or you can live as if everything is a miracle."

—Albert Einstein, physicist, a Pisces

"For all my education, accomplishments, and so-called wisdom, I can't fathom my own heart."

—Michael Caine, actor, a Pisces

"It takes a lot of courage to show your dreams to someone else."

—Erma Bombeck, humorist and author, a Pisces

"I had a child's emotions in a woman's body."

—Elizabeth Taylor, actress, a Pisces

"I can't be funny if my feet don't feel right."

—Billy Crystal, actor, writer, and comedian, a Pisces

YOUR PISCES PERSONALITY

YOUR MOST LIKEABLE TRAIT: Compassion

The bright side of Pisces: Sensitive, loving, nurturing, creative, loyal

The dark side of Pisces: Indecisive, vague, discontented, secretive, easily confused

Pisces is the sign of depths of emotion. It is the last sign of the zodiac, linked to the themes of secrets and sacrifice. You are a deep thinker, interested in things hidden from the eye but not from the heart. You're a gifted psychic, compassionate healer, and inspired artist. With your sensitivity and imagination, you're blessed with creative genius. At the same time, you're strongly pulled toward escaping into fantasy and self-defeating behavior in order to avoid the realities of life. Lacking confidence, you can become far too dependent on others. Curiously, though, you're also a bulwark for those in need. Your nurturing heart reaches out to care for anyone (or anything) suffering pain or lack. But here your tendency is to become self-sacrificing. The Piscean lesson is to find self-power through balance.

Just as the first sign of the zodiac, Aries, represents a new beginning, so the twelfth and last sign, Pisces, is the end of the circle, the sign of eternity, reincarnation, and spiritual rebirth. Many astrologers say that Pisces is a link to the spirit world and that you who are born under this sign are old souls, for they believe Pisceans have experienced other lives in the past.

Pisces has an otherworldly quality. In mystical terms, you are described as half-body and half-spirit, pulled between material existence and spiritual concerns, possessed of the knowledge that you will never be entirely at home in the real world.

Like natives of the other Water signs (Cancer and Scorpio), you are motivated through the senses rather than the intellect. One secret of your extraordinary appeal is your ability to see deeply into the human psyche. Subtle and intuitive, you are born with the gift of prophecy and may even become involved in the occult, ESP, and spiritualism. Because you have a close relationship with astral forces, you feel things before you know them, and your feelings are rarely wrong. If you get a hunch, others would be wise to pay attention. Part of your clairvoyance stems from the fact that you understand first with your heart, and only then do you rationalize what you know intuitively.

Ruled by Neptune, planet of mystery and illusion, your personality is elusive, fey, and quicksilvery. Your element is Water, and the imagery of the sea is evident in how easily you adapt to the ever-shifting currents around you. More than natives of any other sign, you are enormously influenced by your surroundings and by the people who touch your life. Indeed, you have a unique ability to get under another person's skin, to take literally as your own another's problems, joys, and woes. You have tender sympathy for anyone or anything that hurts; sick plants, hungry animals, and friends in need—they all find a home with you. You will give anything asked of you because your desire is to help—and at times you give away the very strength and emotional security you need for yourself.

You possess superb intuitions and a seemingly bottomless understanding of other people, yet your sensitivity can be your most vulnerable point. You are too impressionable to each passing influence, too susceptible to someone else's hard-luck story or plea for help. For you, learning to say no can be a lifetime project, and you may never learn how to do it at all. Whether your feelings are of no self or self-inadequacy or, conversely, self-exaggeration, the core Pisces issue is that of *self*. Your journey is to find a clear self-identity.

Ancient astrologers called Pisces the sign of Sorrow from Self-Undoing, and you can easily become the creator of your own downfall. You are impractical and fall prey to overindulgence. You also have a penchant for picking the wrong companions. A fatal flaw in Pisces is the tendency to flee from what you don't want to deal with, and this can lead you into a world of addictive behavior. At times, your life may become so punctuated with trouble and heartache that you try desperately to escape, and then you are like Eliza jumping from ice floe to ice floe, with no clear sense of where you are headed.

Your symbol, two fishes tied together swimming in opposite directions, represents conflicting emotions and desires that pull you to and fro. You must fight hard for stability, for the strength of purpose and balance needed to combat the negativity of laziness, carelessness, and emotional confusion. You need to develop a positive self-image, play on your strengths and ability to take responsibility, not let yourself fall victim to bad choices and your predilection for self-undoing. Your life lesson is to learn self-*doing*.

Certainly, you do not lack backbone. Indeed, you are capable of great sacrifice and hard work in the service of a cause or an ideal. Intellectually you are curious and like to explore the unusual and hidden. Although you can be impractical, even lazy, you are also capable of prodigious work when you are involved in a project you truly care about. The thing is that, despite the fact you work unselfishly for others, you find it hard to be strict and disciplined with yourself. A Pisces trademark is loss of attention. Even when you're focused, you can be distracted by something unusual, enticing, magical—a moment that sparks a flight of fancy. You've been described as being lost in a funhouse of your own reflections.

Not many natives of this sign are suited to the harsh, tough-and-tumble world of business and commerce. Pisces is the mystical sign of the poet and the dreamer, and you're more successful as a writer, musician, or artist. Intensely imaginative, highly articulate, able to weave a spell with words, you strive to create a world that comes closer to your own unique vision. You're addicted to make-believe, and when you put your energy into creating fantasies, you're the most creative artist in the zodiac.

Because you blend compassion and understanding with great verve, you exert a unique power on people whose lives touch yours. You may feel you lack self-confidence to be a leader, but you are definitely a guide, teacher, and role model to many. You are also a charmer with mischievous wit and a playful sense of humor who loves to laugh. Yet because you are fundamentally unsure of yourself, you prefer to work alone rather than with people. You have an instinct for finding what appears to be the easy way out, and you founder in the shallows of least resistance. This is why so many talented, charming, superior natives of this sign never attain the position in life to which their gifts entitle them.

You are a very special person whose sensitivity and awareness will always appeal to a select group. You are capable of high intellectual achievement, and your magnetic, mysterious, engaging, and delightful personality is heightened by an intriguing sense of drama.

You are also loyal, unselfish, and generous, always ready to help someone who has fallen on hard times. Throughout your life, people will be drawn to you, for you know intuitively how to deal with another's emotions. In fact, you often create a special kind of magic—when you concentrate on the best and reject what is ugly and mean-spirited in people, they are likely to live up to your vision.

You have a wonderful gift for helping others to love themselves, for you have a deep appreciation for their inner qualities. You're not concerned with the superficial and with what people see on the surface. You look at the inner soul, the essence.

There is no more sensitive, perceptive friend than you, nor one more warmhearted, caring, devoted, and sentimental.

THE INNER YOU

You absorb impressions, images, and emotions from everything around you, and then filter them through your rose-colored view of how you'd like things to be. This is not to say you cannot deal with reality—it's just that you like to think of life as an ultra-romantic movie filled with happy endings and where everyone has the best possible motives. You're a big bundle of feelings. You feel intense joy and happiness when you're involved in a creative project or a loving relationship. The opposite is also true: You can suffer greater depths of sadness than most. Yet you're tougher than most people think. Push you down and you keep bouncing back like a rubber bathtub toy. You're charged with energy and get caught up in what's going on around you. Your greatest strength is in giving to others; you're always ready to help whoever needs you.

HOW OTHERS SEE YOU

Everyone thinks you are his or her special friend, that they have your undivided attention. You're thought of as solicitous and concerned. You're also known as a sparkling social presence—witty, vivacious, and always interested in new activities. People consider you artistic and somewhat bohemian and are impressed by your psychic sensibility. They value you as a confidant, but oddly, the more people lean on you, the weaker they think *you* are.

GUARD AGAINST:
Falling Prey to Your Escapist Tendencies

Because Pisces feels things so deeply, you carry a heavy psychic burden. Some people might be able to shrug off gloomy thoughts, deflect a hurtful remark, or turn away from sadness, but you have a way of taking pain into your heart. You're an absorber of feelings. You're particularly susceptible to feeling fear—not the kind that comes from real life but from your imaginings. You think of all the things that can go wrong in a situation and all the worst outcomes. Being intuitive, as well, you pick up on the negativity of others, which makes you feel even more vulnerable.

The Pisces Fish wants to swim away to tranquil waters. You want to escape—and escape comes in many forms. You can flee into fantasy and not deal with reality (e.g., the choices that confront you). You may escape into addictive behavior, using food or alcohol or tranquilizers to dull the senses. You may sleep twelve hours a day. You may escape into other people, hoping they'll shield you from the hard stuff you're facing. Another escape is through denial—insisting that *this* set of circumstances isn't so but *that* one is. How confusing that you who can envision the worst-case scenario can also deny any scenario. But then chaotic thinking is a Piscean specialty.

Taking the easy way out seems so *easy*. But, in fact, it muddies up your life and causes untold heartache—far more struggle than the original struggle you didn't want to deal with in the first place. The truth is that the easy way out is to take responsibility. Pisces, you generally feel you cannot do this (you're not strong enough, you will fail, etc.), but you're among those best suited for responsibility. You're evolved—you're wise in ways others aren't—and you're strong. One of the most important lessons of your life is to find within yourself (in all that inner wisdom) the knowledge of your own power. Pisces doesn't need to escape, for you are superior in intelligence and coping skills. When you can walk away from your excuses and illusions and false promises to yourself that you'll change, you will make extraordinary beginnings that truly alter your life.

YOUR GREATEST CHALLENGE:
To Learn How Not to Be the Victim

You see yourself as being the selfless helper, the one who steps in when others need you, but too often your selflessness turns into allowing yourself to be victimized. You're drawn to the role of the rescuer even at the expense of your own needs. You have a poor sense of boundaries and will use up your own reserves, especially emotional ones. Your personal boundaries are diffuse, and you immerse yourself in the drama of someone else's life. Being impressionable, you can also be gullible, particularly when you don't check out the facts. You want to believe what another is telling you. You'll ignore the fact that what someone is saying or promising is not what his or her behavior is saying. You can be an easy mark. Pisces has a special instinct for attracting codependent relationships—where each enables the other in detrimental behavior. Being the martyr also comes easily to Pisces; you will stay in a bad relationship, taking abuse from an employer, lover, family member, or friend.

All this may sound as if you're ready for the loony bin, which is certainly not what astrology teaches. It tells you that your propensities for feeling deeply and being the one who's most self-sacrificing can lead you into the shallows of life. Your unhealthiest tendency is to disbelieve yourself—and your healthiest drive is to nurture. By making choices that strengthen your individuality and self-confidence, and wisely selecting worthy recipients for your nurturing (e.g., people who give back to you as much as they get, creative projects that express your true imaginative spirit), you will never be the victim.

YOUR ALTER EGO

Astrology gives us many tools in our lives to help manage our struggles and solve problems. One of these tools is to reach into your opposite sign in the zodiac—your polarity.

For you, Pisces, this is Virgo, sign of work, productivity, and utilizing talents. Virgo is industrious and organized and, possessing high intelligence, able to distinguish what is valuable and useful from what is not. Virgo's great gift is to create perfection. Of course, nothing is totally perfect, but Virgo's way is to give all its attention and service to making the task, project, or enterprise as first-rate as possible.

What Pisces and Virgo share is the inclination to *serve*. Both of you are givers who need to be needed. The difference is in how you serve. Virgo is the practical doer who knows the most efficient method and is the fixer. Pisces is the emotional nurturer who steps in to give comfort and healing. If the two of you were missionaries, Virgo would be the educator who teaches a useful trade and Pisces would be the physician who treats the sick and injured.

Pisces and Virgo are both Mutable signs, and therefore flexible. Virgo is open to experimentation in order to find the best method of achieving goals. Particularly, Virgo looks for actual results—this is definitely the sign of being pragmatic. Mutable Pisces is also flexible, but your adaptability is to people. You adjust to others' moods and desires and what they want of you.

You, Pisces, can benefit from adopting some of Virgo's focus on discipline and order. By tapping into Virgo's concentration on self-improvement, you'll counteract the Piscean leaning toward self-undoing. Down-to-earth, diligent, and reliable, Virgo is able to control its environment. If you follow Virgo's example of setting high standards and using intellectual vigor, you can be a serene achiever—*serene* meaning not continually fighting against chaos, confusion, and distraction. Virgo can teach you self-control and dealing with life logically. Especially, you can utilize the Virgo capacity to see the difference between what is healthy and unhealthy and therefore make positive choices.

In turn, Virgo has much to learn from you, and at the top of the list is how to break out of the stricture of narrow thinking. You're blessed with the power of imagination. You're able to visualize what is possible, not just probable. Unlike you, Virgo can never rise to greatness unless it can get beyond the boundaries of "this is right, this is so." You, Pisces, want to go beyond; you're brilliantly intuitive, and your mind is a rich tapestry. Virgo can learn from you that side paths often lead to treasure, that making a leap of faith can produce miracles, and that asking the question "what if?" will bring answers from the universe. In addition, Virgo needs to open its heart the way you do. Virgo tends to be critical and exacting, whereas you have empathy and compassion. Because you're able to feel others' feelings, you're accepting of people with their flaws and foibles. You have the boundless quality that marks a great spiritual adviser.

PISCES IN LOVE

You are a fascinating mixture of earthly passion and unworldly fantasies. You have an indefinable magnetism, a bewitching quality. It's no wonder that you captivate those who want to plumb the depths of your enticing allure.

Like the other Water signs (Cancer and Scorpio), you have a mysterious way of uncovering the secrets that lie beneath a person's social mask. You're exceptionally sensitive to the slightest nuance in what someone says or how someone behaves—which makes the person feel you can read his or her heart. At the same time, Pisces tends to project superlative qualities onto that person. Therefore, he or she is totally enchanted not only to feel known by you, but to be known as wonderful.

All the Water signs have the quality of emotional imagination. Cancer uses it to create a protective environment; Scorpio seeks to delve into the secrets of the human psyche. Pisces tries to live in a world of dreams and romance. You want to unite in an almost mystical communion in love. You want to enter into the psyche of your love.

You are intensely emotional about making love because you consider it not a merely physical act but the culmination of a romantic yearning. You have deeply erotic passions, and your bedroom behavior inclines toward the offbeat and uninhibited. You're innovative and sensuous—in many ways a mind-and-body reader finely attuned to a partner's unspoken desires. Your sexual intuitions are almost psychic.

The lovers you choose tend to fall into extremes. Because you need to be needed, you're attracted to emotionally handicapped partners whom you can nurture and protect and envelop. You also fall in love with the opposite kind of person—someone strong, decisive, and sure of himself or herself, someone who can provide support and firm direction. If you are a Pisces woman, you particularly want to fall in love with a hero who can take care of you emotionally and financially. Yet it's *you* who assigns heroic qualities to the man; it's an illusion you create. And the irony is that the men who are dominant and high-powered are the very ones who will make you feel most alone.

If you are a Pisces man, you have rare charisma. The power of your seduction is you go right to a woman's soul, and nothing in the world is more beguiling. Much as you want to connect on a soul-level, though, your nature is to be unconfined; you keep swimming away. Indeed, it's been said that in every woman's past there is a Pisces man. While the romantic moment lasts, you can make it seem enchanted, everything a lover ever dreamed of, champagne and caviar, moonlight and poetry and passion. Unfortunately, when the sun comes up, the words don't quite rhyme and the champagne is flat. You would like to find happiness with one woman, but the vagaries of your character and the constant appeal of change make this unlikely. You find it hard to steer a steady course between your conflicting desires.

All Pisceans fall in love easily, yet you can be unlucky in love because you tend to lose your mind to an illusion. Sacrifice is a major theme in your love life. The first step is you sacrifice your reasoning powers. Then if you're deeply into a dysfunctional relationship, you sacrifice your dream. You become the classic martyr, sacrificing yourself and enabling a partner you feel cannot survive without you.

Longing is also a huge element in your relationships. Pisces is drawn to unrequited love, or doomed affairs (with someone married, for example), or obsessive memories of a long-lost love. Fatal attractions are a Piscean specialty—clandestine meetings and secret relationships with high-risk quotients. Your love life tends to be chaotic and turbulent. You're attracted to danger, yet emotionally, your deepest need is for security (another example of the two fishes swimming in opposite directions). Yours is the sign of self-undoing, and over your lifetime you may lose your heart many times to the wrong partner.

Yet when magic happens and you truly give your heart to a soulmate, the best in you expands and multiplies. With love at the center, no one else can make romance seem as enchanted as you can. You're a person of warmth and compassion who will cherish and nurture your partner and do all you can to make your mate happy. You give unselfishly of your time, energy, sympathy, and concern. Your affections are undivided, and your loyalty is deep and strong. What you seek from a lover is perfect unity, and you will make great personal sacrifices to achieve the best for the one you love.

TIPS FOR THOSE WHO WANT TO ATTRACT PISCES

You can always interest them in conversation about the world of entertainment, art, books, poetry, and drama. Another sure way to get their attention is to discuss any topic touching on the occult, mysticism, spiritualism, and the supernatural, particularly anything involving reincarnation. Pisceans who don't actually believe in it (there aren't many) are fascinated by discussions about it.

Tell them your problems. They're great listeners and their sympathy is mostly genuine. But avoid giving the appearance of being overwhelmed by your problems. While Pisceans have an unusual compassion for losers, they prefer people who are strong and supportive, with definite goals and a positive approach to life.

A good compromise tactic is to discuss your difficulties humorously. Pisceans like to laugh and will be impressed by your ability to smile your troubles away.

Ask them about a subject they know well. (Tip: Pisceans are artistic, or at least have a real appreciation for the arts, so you can hardly go wrong moving in that direction.) Pisces will soon open up. In fact, your problem may be getting back in control of the conversation. Pisceans love to expound and explain and expatiate.

Always greet them with a compliment about their appearance or social presence, or remember to repeat a flattering comment someone else made about them. Pisces soaks up flattery like the Sahara soaks up water.

Above all, be sentimental. Remember each birthday and anniversary. Pisceans are grateful, and they don't forget kindness or thoughtfulness. You'll be richly rewarded.

....

PISCES'S EROGENOUS ZONES:
Tips for Those with a Pisces Lover

....

Our bodies are very sensitive to the touch of another human being. The special language of touching is understood on a level more basic than speech. Each sign is linked to certain zones and areas of the body that are especially receptive and can receive sexual message through touch. Many books and manuals have been written about lovemaking, but few pay attention to the unique knowledge of erogenous zones supplied by astrology. You can use astrology to become a better, more sensitive lover.

For Pisces, the feet are the special area that is sensitive to erotic touch. The practice of reflexology is based on a school of thought that maintains that the foot represents the body in microcosm— that different parts of the foot correspond to various parts of the body. Thus, massaging, touching, and treating different parts of the foot can stimulate and treat the whole body. If this theory is valid, it should be particularly true for Pisces.

You can use massage on Pisces's feet both to induce relaxation and to increase sexual desire. Here is a relaxing technique: (1) Grasp all five toes and bend them toward and then away from the ankle. Repeat ten times. (2) Using thumbs and fingers, knead and rub the soles of the feet. Knead the top of the foot, using lighter pressure. (3) Gently pinch and knead the Achilles tendon. (4) Grasp the foot with both hands and gently wring, starting near the toes and working up to the ankle.

The best beginning to an erotic massage is a foot soak in warm, scented water. Follow up with an application of skin lotion all over the feet and toes, paying special attention to the soles of the feet and to the skin between the toes. Then, using just fingertips or fingernails, gently caress the heel and arch. At the anklebone, use a featherlight circular motion with your fingertips. Move around to the top of the foot and then down to the toes. If you rub Pisces's toes between the pads of your fingers, you will send a very definite sexual message.

Pisceans often use their feet to enhance the act of love. Pisces woman will gently masturbate her lover using the balls of her feet. Male Pisces gets added stimulation by rubbing his feet over the vaginal area.

PISCES'S AMOROUS COMBINATIONS: YOUR LOVE PARTNERS

PISCES AND ARIES

You're deeply sensual and are drawn to Aries's dynamic passions. In turn, your desire to shower affection on a lover flatters Aries. Your Pisces imagination and mysterious allure bring out a new sensitivity and romanticism in Aries, who can be an aggressive lover. Pisces and Aries both need attention, which you give to each other in different ways. You are abundantly affectionate, and Aries likes to handle decisions and fight battles for you. This is just what you're looking for. Headstrong Aries will dominate, but this doesn't necessarily displease you—you like to have someone to lean on. What will trouble you more is Aries's tendency to criticize. Your feelings are easily hurt, and Aries is the one to tread all over them. Tact is needed to cement this otherwise sexy partnership.

PISCES AND TAURUS

Taurus is a strong, authoritative figure who can provide stability for you. Pisces tends to be vacillating, changeable, and needs a lot of TLC, and happily Taurus is the solid, dependable one who dotes on you. Taurus's artistic bent enhances your creative imagination, while you are very supportive of Taurus's ambitions. You also accentuate Taurus's taste for comfort, and together you'll furnish a luxurious setting for love. Both Pisces and Taurus are highly passionate and sensual—and you, Pisces, add a touch of erotic fantasy to your lovemaking. However, you are more volatile and emotional than Taurus, and although Taurus's possessiveness makes you feel secure, Taurus can be a bit too practical and down-to-earth to satisfy your Piscean romantic nature. If you two can work out this problem, all goes well.

PISCES AND GEMINI

You're drawn to Gemini's wit and communicativeness, and Gemini is fascinated by your mystery. Early on you strike sexual sparks because Gemini loves experimentation and is captivated by your willing eroticism. Unfortunately, this combination is as unstable as nitroglycerin—and likely to blow up. You can't stand Gemini's fickleness and thoughtlessness. Gemini can't stand your emotionalism and dreaminess. Piscean insecurities make you possessive and clinging, but Gemini wants to have fun and move on. You look for love to be a sanctuary, while Gemini wants it to be in a perfect state of freedom. In different ways, you're each as shifting and changeable as the other. Pisces lacks direction, while Gemini goes off in too many directions. Each is also very self-absorbed, and you both need more dominant partners.

PISCES AND CANCER

You two immediately discover emotional and psychic rapport—you're both Water signs who seduce each other with your warmth and sensitivity. You even think alike. You quickly become a romantic duo that finds passion and tenderness in each other. You, Pisces, especially revel in Cancer's sexual demands, for Cancer is as sensual as you and the erotic union you have together makes you feel intensely bonded. Also, both of you are able to communicate feelings, a big plus in your relationship. You don't mind if Cancer makes most of the decisions; Cancer's concern for security and excellent money sense provide a very practical stability. You both are sentimental types who like to stick close to home. Loyal Cancer devotes itself exclusively to you, and in turn, you idolize Cancer. A very compatible pair.

PISCES AND LEO

Your tendency to think rather than act annoys Leo, who considers you wishy-washy. You two are very unalike: Pisces is shy, introverted, and vulnerable, while Leo is arrogant, brash, and domineering. Leo is initially spellbound by your ultrasensuality, but a brief sexual fascination with each other soon evaporates. Both of you behave emotionally, but Leo is given to temperamental outbursts while you withdraw into private fantasy. Leo won't tolerate your sensitivity and dreaminess. Highly social Leo seeks lots of attention and feedback, while you demand exclusivity. Leo likes to roam; Pisces doesn't. Leo is enormously self-centered and takes you entirely for granted. Indeed, neither of you has an inkling what the other needs. This combination is like fire and water—they don't mix.

PISCES AND VIRGO

Your affectionate nature intrigues Virgo at first, but your personalities are just too opposite for any rapport. Virgo, being a mental sign, distrusts emotions, whereas you run your life emotionally rather than intellectually. Reserved, faultfinding Virgo won't satisfy you sexually, and when the Virgo sexual rebuffs begin, this awakens your Piscean insecurities. Virgo also can't give you the romance or ego bolstering you need, and your predilection for building dream castles and following your creative whims proves to be too unstable for exacting Virgo. Virgo will resent your need for tenderness and intimacy, which it sees as overdependency. You're both communicators, but Pisces speaks of deep feelings and Virgo deals with facts and information and tells you how to shape up. This relationship soon becomes a toboggan to nowhere.

PISCES AND LIBRA

Both of you are affectionate, creative, artistic people who take to each other immediately. But Pisces is looking for emotional support and won't find this with airy Libra, who is not a strong center. You want love to be deep and transcendent, whereas Libra has a more Hollywood-movie view of love. Libra delights in romance and harmony but flees from the responsibility of any kind of demands or entanglements. You both like luxury and a lovely home, but Pisces is too lazy about making money and Libra is too extravagant about spending it. Libra has numerous outside interests and feels stifled by you. Basically, this relationship is unfair because you end up being the giver, and Libra is the taker. Sexual rapport isn't enough for the long term. But as long as it lasts, this can be fun if you don't ask for too much.

PISCES AND SCORPIO

Immediately, your chemistry together is visible for all to see. You quickly ignite as lovers, and with Scorpio you find your match—and then some. Scorpio provides a deep, exciting sexual union for you and gives you valuable emotional support, strength, and leadership. Both of you seek security and have the capacity to become profoundly attached. The sweet, seductive way you melt into a relationship is just what Scorpio is looking for—and Scorpio's jealousy and possessiveness won't bother you. In fact, they make you feel loved. You two share a special communion, much of it on a sensual, unspoken level. You both have intense feelings and are loyal, intuitive, and interested in the mystical and the unusual. Pisces is a creative dreamer and Scorpio a great accomplisher, and as a team you blend many talents. An ideal mating.

PISCES AND SAGITTARIUS

At the start, you're enlivened by Sagittarius's charm and enthusiasm, and Sagittarius is mesmerized by your sensuality. You two ignite in the bedroom, but the compatibility ends there. You're an imaginative dreamer, whereas Sagittarius thrives on constant activity. Independent Sagittarius is too much of a rover to satisfy your need for attention and devotion. Both of you tend to be unreliable—Sagittarius flees toward new escapades, and Pisces withdraws into fantasy. Sagittarius can't resist poking fun and provoking, and its sharp tongue will hurt your sentimental feelings. You seek intimacy and communion, but are constantly confused and rebuffed by Sagittarius's struggle to free itself of emotional demands. You want to create a love nest at home, but restless, adventurous Sagittarius won't stay home long.

PISCES AND CAPRICORN

You are two very different people who please each other. Capricorn's strong, dominant personality is just what you need. You feel secure with down-to-earth, determined Capricorn, who can take charge and make decisions and teach you to be more practical. In turn, you bring a touch of poetic beauty and a breath of romance to Capricorn's staid approach to life. Your lavishness with praise and affection delights Capricorn; you know how to stroke Capricorn's ego in just the right way. Capricorn does not easily verbalize its feelings, but you intuitively recognize Capricorn's loyalty and devotion. Sexually, you two find depth and intensity together. Capricorn has robustly earthy passions that make you feel desirable. As a couple, your contrasting temperaments neatly complement each other.

PISCES AND AQUARIUS

Your Piscean romantic eroticism inspires Aquarius to experiment in new areas. Sexually, this might be fun since you're both venturesome in entirely different ways. But Aquarius is detached, interested in ideas and the world at large, while you are interested in sensual fulfillment and exploring the wilder shores of love. The vast chasm between Pisces and Aquarius is that you perceive the world through your emotions and Aquarius filters everything through its mind. You're the romantic who gives yourself to one soulmate, whereas Aquarius is the humanitarian who cares for people in general but has trouble caring for one person in particular. Eventually, outgoing and social-minded Aquarius will start looking around, and Pisces can't endure that. Independent Aquarius needs freedom and after a while resents your struggle to keep Aquarius caged at home.

PISCES AND PISCES

You two draw into a compelling coming-together, sometimes from across a crowded room. You share mutual sympathy and intuition and a romantic approach to life. Sexually, you combine in a mystical, poetic way filled with profound eroticism. And if all your problems could be resolved in the bedroom, yours would be one of the zodiac's best matches. Alas, you both need what the other does not have. Each tends to be weak-willed and dependent and drains the other emotionally. Both of you have a tendency to sink into a mire of self-pity and negativity. You accentuate each other's confusion, self-indulgence, and muddled thinking. Pisces finds it hard to cope with practical realities, and there's no strong partner around to push either of you in the right direction. This sexy affair has no place to go.

YOUR PISCES CAREER PATH

Pisces is the sign of imagination and fantasy, and these qualities are the starting point of your career path and the cornerstones of your work. Whether you begin on the lowest rung of a tedious job or land into exactly what you're looking for, your career is fueled by your dreams and fantasies. One of your big Pisces lessons, however, is that your dreams remain dreams unless you make them a reality—and that this is *your* job to do. No one is going to do this for you.

Of all the signs, you're blessed with the most creative imagination. You're the artist, poet, musician, mystic, and philosopher, the one with a spiritual nature. You have ambition, but generally not for what many want—climbing to the top of the corporate world, being a celebrity, marrying into wealth. Certainly, having enough money makes you feel secure, but fierce competitiveness and ruthlessness are not your dominant traits. Early in life you may even think you lack strength or are untalented, neither of which is true. (Beware your number one obstacle: lack of faith in yourself.) You have *extraordinary* talent, and you can be focused. But you, Pisces Fish, must be brave enough to swim into the currents of creativity. This is the secret to tapping into your career power.

Remember, to *create* means to give rise to, to produce, to bring something into being.

Happily, you do have cosmic timing on your side—the universe seems to love someone as exceptional as you. A magic door always opens (e.g., you meet the right person or a string of events pushes you into a lucky situation). Pisces, pay attention to the synchronicity around you—and definitely say yes. As tends to happen with out-of-work actors, saying yes to a role that isn't quite your cup of tea can lead to the role that's perfect for you.

Flexibility is a Piscean trademark, and you need a schedule that gives you this. Having a modicum of structure and routine is ideal, for these constructive tools give you parameters. However, your Piscean creative spirit will be totally deadened if your work does not allow you to think out of the box, try new things, set your own pace, and give you opportunity for self-expression. Security is important, but steer away from an occupation that makes you feel claustrophobic.

Variety and diversity are vital requirements in your work so that you can experiment and flow. But you must also be careful not to flow away and disappear. Among the most crucial elements you need is *direction*. You must keep to your direction; you must discipline yourself to stay on course and not swim off into distractions. In addition, you benefit from taking direction (not to be confused with taking orders). Taking direction is something you do extremely well—you always gain enormously from a mentor or wise adviser. In addition, you do successful work teamed with someone disciplined and knowledgeable. You supply ideas and inspiration, and the other person supplies organization (not your strong suit) and clear guidance.

As a Piscean, you're gifted in a myriad of areas. It goes almost without saying that the world of the arts calls to you. You can act, write, dance, perform, make films, sculpt, paint, create music. Books, literature, playwriting, and scriptwriting are special Piscean fields. You have a superb eye for design and color and do well in fashion, interior decorating, cosmetology, modeling, photography. You're also pulled toward the helping professions, such as medicine, nursing, psychology, teaching, social work, drug and alcohol counseling, physical therapy, and rehabilitation work. Pisces is a Water sign, and a career in the nautical sphere fits you. You're very spiritual and can make a profound impact in religious, charitable, and humanitarian work. With your Piscean sixth sense, you can be a gifted medium, psychic, or astrologer.

For Pisces, work must be something you wholly invest yourself in emotionally. Your most compelling endeavors are those in which you lose yourself. You are capable of achieving any goal on which you set your heart—and all you have to do is get out of your own way. Negative Piscean proclivities, such as indecision, procrastination, or daydreaming time away, will halt you in your tracks. But when you focus and make use of your abundant skills, you are in a powerful flow and your work will have a luminous purity. You can *create*.

PISCES AND HEALTH:
ADVICE FROM ASTROLOGY

You are a sensitive person, emotionally and physically, and easily affected by what comes at you (for example, stressful situations, contagious germs, etc.). You must put up strong defenses by maintaining a healthy lifestyle. You need quality nutrition, exercise, and proper sleep. You're particularly susceptible to alcohol and drugs (which can include many over-the-counter drugs) and must pay close attention to your body's intolerance to toxic substances. As a Pisces, your feet are especially vulnerable, and you're prone to foot ailments, bunions, blisters, and nerve damage. It's important to wear comfortable, well-fitting shoes and to take extra care in how you treat your feet and how you look after their health. You also need periods of time for yourself to unwind, create, and reflect on relationships and events in your life.

Advice and useful tips about health are among the most important kinds of information that astrology provides. Health and well-being are of paramount concern to human beings. Love, money, or career takes second place, for without good health we cannot enjoy anything in life.

Astrology and medicine have had a long marriage. Hippocrates (born around 460 B.C.), the Greek philosopher and physician who is considered the father of medicine, said, "A physician without a knowledge of astrology has no right to call himself a physician." Indeed, up until the eighteenth century, the study of astrology and its relationship to the body was very much a part of a doctor's training. When a patient became ill, a chart was immediately drawn up. This guided the doctor in both diagnosis and treatment, for the chart would tell when the crisis would come and what medicine would help. Of course, modern Western doctors no longer use astrology to treat illness. However, astrology can still be a useful tool in helping to understand and maintain our physical well-being.

THE PART OF THE BODY RULED BY PISCES

Each sign of the zodiac governs a specific part of the body. These associations date back to the beginning of astrology. Curiously, the part of the body that a sign rules is in some ways the strongest and in other ways the weakest area for natives of that sign.

Your sign of Pisces rules the feet and toes and the mucous membranes. Pisceans are noted for their graceful, well-shaped feet, and many become excellent dancers. Your sense of taste and smell are exceptionally acute. In general, health is not robust in Pisces. You tend to have a delicate constitution that does not easily fight off disease. You're vulnerable to colds and sinus trouble, and you need lots of rest to keep your vitality. You're prone to water retention in the body. You have a sensitive, emotional personality, and illness is frequently emotionally based. Depression, too, is something Pisces is prone toward.

The feet tend to be a source of trouble for Pisceans. You find it difficult to do work that requires long hours of standing. You may suffer from corns and bunions. Ill-fitting shoes are particularly troublesome, for you're likely to have difficulty finding shoes that will properly fit your sensitive feet. You usually kick off your shoes at the first opportunity and walk in slippers or barefooted. You're prone to athlete's foot and other fungus infections, such as toenail fungus. Gout often afflicts the toes. Bruised, stubbed, or broken toes are also common injuries to Pisceans.

Neptune, the planet that rules Pisces, acts on the general nervous system and specifically on the thalamus. The thalamus is the part of the brain that transmits stimuli and motor signals to and from the sensory organs.

As a Pisces, you're especially sensitive to stimuli around you. You're very impressionable and often involved in creative work, music, art, and drama. Unfortunately, Pisces people can easily fall prey to the influence of alcohol and drugs. You must be careful, too, when taking medicine (even something as common as aspirin), and carefully monitor your body's reactions to any kind of medical drug.

DIET AND HEALTH TIPS FOR PISCES

Pisceans are attracted to glamorous living, which often includes overindulging in eating and drinking and keeping late hours. The key to your good health is to establish moderate habits. With a minimum of care—a well-balanced diet, moderate exercise, rest— you can feel younger than you are and keep your good looks well into old age.

Pisces's cell salt* is ferrum phosphate, which is iron. Iron is needed for the manufacture of hemoglobin in the bloodstream. Hemoglobin is the essential element in the red blood cell and is responsible for the transport of oxygen from the lungs to other body cells. Lack of iron in the system leads to anemia, low blood pressure, inflammations, glandular problems, and heart irregularities.

Foods rich in iron that you should include in your diet are lean beef, lamb, egg yolks, oysters, kidneys, whole-grain cereals, barley, dried beans, beet tops, spinach, onions, lettuce, raisins, dates, prunes, apricots, peaches, grapes, apples, lemons, and oranges. You function best with a high-protein diet that is low in fat and sugar. Lean broiled meat, chicken, fish, natural cheeses, yogurt, and nuts are excellent sources of protein. You should cut down on table salt, for this causes bloating (something you're quite prone to). Caffeine overstimulates you and should be cut down to a bare minimum.

Pisceans are particularly susceptible to the effects of alcohol, which will age you quicker than anyone else in the zodiac. In addition, overindulgence in alcohol can quickly lead to depression. Caution: Drugs and medicine should be taken only under the supervision of a doctor.

You need lots of rest to keep up vitality, which tends to be on the low side. Wonderful exercises are swimming and dancing; both will keep you fit and glowing. You should take extra care of your feet and wear comfortable, well-fitting shoes. A warm footbath before going to bed will aid relaxation and a good night's sleep. You should never walk around with wet feet or sit on the beach in a wet bathing suit.

---

*Cell salts (also known as tissue salts) are mineral compounds found in human tissue cells. These minerals are the only substances our cells cannot produce by themselves. The life of cells is relatively short, and the creation of new cells depends on the presence of these minerals.

THE DECANATES AND CUSPS OF PISCES

Decanate and *cusp* are astrological terms that subdivide your Sun sign. These subdivisions further define and emphasize certain qualities and character traits of your Sun sign, Pisces.

WHAT IS A DECANATE?

Each astrological sign is divided into three parts, and each part is called a *decanate* or a *decan* (the terms are used interchangeably).

The word comes from the Greek word *dekanoi*, meaning "ten days apart." The Greeks took their word from the Egyptians, who divided their year into 360 days.* The Egyptian year had twelve months of thirty days each, and each month was further divided into three sections of ten days each. It was these ten-day sections the Greeks called *dekanoi*.

---

*The Egyptians soon found out that a 360-day year was inaccurate and so added on five extra days. These were feast days and holidays, and not counted as real days.

Astrology still divides the zodiac into decanates. There are twelve signs in the zodiac, and each sign is divided into three decanates. You might picture each decanate as a room. You were born in the sign of Pisces, which consists of three rooms (decanates). In which room of Pisces were you born?

The zodiac is a 360-degree circle. Each decanate is ten degrees of that circle, or about ten days long, since the Sun moves through the zodiac at approximately the rate of one degree per day. (This is not exact because not all of our months contain thirty days.)

The decanate of a sign does not change the basic characteristics of that sign, but it does refine and individualize the sign's general characteristics. If you were born, say, in the second decanate of Pisces, it does not change the fact you are a Piscean. It does indicate that you have somewhat different and special characteristics from those Piscean people born in the first decanate or the third decanate.

Finally, each decanate has a specific planetary ruler, sometimes called a subruler because it does not usurp the overall rulership of your sign. The subruler can only enhance and add to the distinct characteristics of your decanate. For example, your entire sign of Pisces is ruled by Neptune, but the second decanate of Pisces is subruled by the Moon. The influence of the Moon, the subruler, combines with the overall authority of Neptune to make the second decanate of Pisces unlike any other in the zodiac.

FIRST DECANATE OF PISCES

February 19 through February 29

Keyword: Imagination

Constellation: Pegasus, the Winged Horse who bears the rider of good fortune.

Planetary Subruler: Neptune

Neptune, planet of illusion, is both your ruler and subruler, which emphasizes creativity and imagination. There may be involvement in artistic or literary work; you have a talent for expressing your inner thoughts. You are particularly sensitive to the people with whom you share your life. Discord is unbearable to you, and you will do your best to shield yourself from unpleasantness. Your keen mind is open to ideas, and personal achievement is important to you. Often you must struggle to accentuate positives instead of letting negative feelings overwhelm you. You may suffer from physical ailments, but your character is very strong. Love is probably tempestuous, for you have deep passions.

SECOND DECANATE OF PISCES

March 1 through March 10

Keyword: Compassion

Constellation: Cygnus, the Swan. Also called the Northern Cross. The Swan is the celestial symbol of grace and beauty.

Planetary Subruler: Moon

The receptive Moon combines with the spiritual influence of Neptune and heightens your awareness of others. You have an uncanny way of knowing what those around you think or feel and can use this power on a much wider scale. You are, or have the potential to become, well known not only in your circle but in the larger world. Your observations are keen; you are able to gather ideas or art forms and transform them with your own unique vision. Social occasions enable you to display your special charm with people and a knack for witty conversation that is one of your strong points. You are a romantic at heart, and love is a transforming experience. Unfortunately, you don't find love easy to hold on to.

THIRD DECANATE OF PISCES

March 11 through March 20
Keyword: Action
Constellation: Cepheus, the Monarch who rests one foot on the Pole Star. He symbolizes constancy.
Planetary Subruler: Pluto

Pluto, planet of power, gives force to Pisces's Neptune and underlines your need for activity and outlets. You possess imagination and vision; if you harness your energy, you can soar to great heights of achievement. Intellectually, you are curious and like to explore the unusual or hidden. You are especially drawn to religious, spiritual, or occult matters. Solitude and periods of withdrawal from others are necessary for you to think, review, and meditate. You have a talent for writing or speaking that can move and influence other people. Your emotions are deep and strong; you understand first with your heart and only then with your head. Love motivates many of your decisions.

WHAT IS A CUSP?

A cusp is the point at which a new astrological sign begins.* Thus, the cusp of Pisces means the point at which Pisces begins. (The word comes from the Latin word *cuspis*, meaning "point.")

When someone speaks of being "born on the cusp," that person is referring to a birth time at or near the beginning or the end of an astrological sign. For example, if you were born on March 20, you were born on the cusp of Aries, the sign that begins on March 21. Indeed, depending on what year you were born, your birth time might even be in the first degree of Aries. People born on the very day a sign begins or ends are often confused about what sign they really are—a confusion made more complicated by the fact that the Sun does not move into or out of a sign at *exactly* the same moment (or even day) each year. There are slight time differences from year to year. Therefore, if you are a Piscean born on February 19 or March 20, you'll find great clarity consulting a computer chart that tells you exactly where the Sun was at the very moment you were born.

As for what span of time constitutes being born on the cusp, the astrological community holds various opinions. Some astrologers claim cusp means being born only within the first two days or last two days of a sign (though many say this is too narrow a time frame). Others say it can be as much as within the first ten days or last ten days of a sign (which many say is too wide an interpretation). The consensus is that you were born on the cusp if your birthday is within the first *five* days or last *five* days of a sign.

*In a birth chart, a cusp is also the point at which an astrological House begins.

The question hanging over cusp-born people is "What sign am I really?" They feel they straddle the border of two different countries. To some extent, this is true. If you were born on the cusp, you're under the influence of both signs. However, much like being a traveler leaving one country and crossing into another, you must actually *be* in one country—you can't be in two countries at the same time. One sign is always a stronger influence, and that sign is almost invariably the sign that the Sun was actually in (in other words, your Sun sign). The reason I say "almost" is that in rare cases a chart may be so heavily weighted with planets in a certain sign that the person more keenly feels the influence of that specific sign.

For example, I have a client who was born in the late evening on March 20. On that evening, the Sun was leaving Pisces and entering Aries. At the moment of her birth, the Sun was still in Pisces, so technically speaking she is a Piscean. However, the Sun was only a couple hours away from being in Aries, and this person has the Moon, Mercury, and Venus all in Aries. She has always felt like an Aries and always behaved as an Aries.

This, obviously, is an unusual case. Generally, the Sun is the most powerful planetary influence in a chart. Even if you were born with the Sun on the very tip of the first or last degree of Pisces, Pisces is your Sun sign—and this is the sign you will most feel like.

Still, the influence of the approaching sign or of the sign just ending is present, and you will probably sense that mixture in yourself.

BORN FEBRUARY 19 THROUGH FEBRUARY 23

You are Pisces with Aquarius tendencies. You have an elegant and refined nature, and also an infectious sense of fun. You possess both determination and good organizational ability, and generally are successful at making money. In your work, you can be incisive and objective about solving problems. People are often surprised at the variety and extent of your interests. You have strong likes and dislikes, but also an open mind that enjoys toying with new ideas. You need change in scenery to keep from becoming bored. Love may be elusive because you need a special kind of person to fulfill you.

BORN MARCH 16 THROUGH MARCH 20

You are Pisces with Aries tendencies. You have keen powers of observation and are drawn to the unusual in people and in ideas. You have a strong personality that makes an impact, and you possess the ability to execute personal plans in spite of obstacles. In short, you are a most original person. You have learned that luck comes when you least expect it. You have a magnetic social touch and are usually surrounded by friends and acquaintances. You are flirtatious and changeable, but in love you are capable of intense devotion.

YOUR SPECIAL DAY OF BIRTH

FEBRUARY 19

You're a born caregiver but have learned to be strong for yourself as well. You have an exuberant love for life and all its experiences. In work, you're able to direct others and lead—and in love, you're softhearted and bountiful and deeply sensual.

FEBRUARY 20

You're logical and rational, and you also have a truly loving heart that is sensitive to others. Your special career talent is to see the larger vision and find new methods. Romantically, you abandon yourself to love and easily fall into tempestuous relationships.

FEBRUARY 21

Piscean duality defines you. You're torn between lazy self-indulgence and stoic self-control. When you get it together, no one is more creative and productive. As for love, you're an affectionate pussycat who adores romantic magic and ecstatic sex.

FEBRUARY 22

Courageous and charismatic, you also fight personal demons of self-indulgent cravings and taking the easy way out. People can't pigeonhole your talents because they are so varied. In love, you're vulnerable, and your lesson is to learn to value your own heart.

FEBRUARY 23

Once you commit yourself, you're able to channel your intense passion into major accomplishment. You're kind and well meaning but can be maddeningly stubborn. In love, your great strength is to endure the low points and come back fighting for the relationship.

FEBRUARY 24

With your magnetism, you have great stage presence, though you'd rather withdraw and do your own thing without interference. You're also a rebel who tends to make unexpected choices—especially in relationships. When you fall into lust, your control crumbles.

FEBRUARY 25

Everyone you know could describe you to some degree but not wholly. You have many facets and special skills. You're motivated by being truthful and finding security—and are promised financial security later in life. You also know how to love unselfishly.

FEBRUARY 26

Your gaze is fixed on long-term stability, but finding this tends to be erratic. You want passion and excitement though you actually feel freer when you take a disciplined approach, especially in work. Emotionally, you express love by becoming the one who serves.

FEBRUARY 27

You have a profound effect on others, though you're unaware of it. Everything you do comes straight from your magnanimous heart—what most people say about you is you're *real*. You're a giver and at your most vibrant with strong relationships of love and support.

FEBRUARY 28

You're a charmer and a communicator. You're quick thinking and wise, and you generally hide your own troubles under a cheery demeanor. You're also ambitious, though you tend to sublimate what you want to others' needs. Love is challenging, for you're a great romantic who can make unrealistic choices.

FEBRUARY 29

Born on a rare day, you're special in the zodiac. You have unusual talents that set you apart. Your heart is like a wandering gypsy, but you will find your "home," creatively and in love. You're complicated, passionate, capable of extraordinary commitment.

MARCH 1

Great panache is your trademark. In all you do, you make an impression on an audience, for your life will always play out in public. In relationships, you're tenacious and passionate—and in love, especially, you swing between being self-indulgent and self-sacrificing.

MARCH 2

Imbued with an explorative spirit, you take chances for which the universe always rewards you. You've learned to trust your own instincts. You have an authoritative personality though you think you're a wimp. In love, your wild heart leads you into unusual byways.

MARCH 3

You have a keen intellect and are patient, but you will suddenly make an impulsive decision. You're driven by a quest to experience more, to find true happiness; the impulses to be safe and be adventurous both exist in you. In love, you're fiercely loyal and have strong sexuality.

MARCH 4

You're organized in your *mind*, even if not about stuff. In work, you need freedom to go your own way—and in life, you're deeply connected to friendships and family. You can be emotionally demanding when feeling insecure in love, yet you are devoted and abundantly sensual.

MARCH 5

You have a talent for motivating others, though you're often at a crossroads about what *you* want. Your strength is your tremendous willpower, and when you stop seeking approval, you can be bold indeed. Love is a challenge, for you want independence and total closeness.

MARCH 6

You don't know how strong you are, how brilliant in your thinking and compelling in your magnetism. Little by little, you're freeing yourself of a difficult past. You're loyal and utterly fair in emotional relationships; be careful about becoming trapped by needy lovers.

MARCH 7

True, you can be moody, but you're also expressive, outgoing, and have unusual people skill. Work is your true center; it grounds you and keeps you sane. You're passionate and can easily become addicted to sex, though in a fulfilling relationship you have a constant heart.

MARCH 8

With your lively grace and sense of humor, you charm people. You hang back from being pushy, but you know you have remarkable talents. In love, you're compassionate and an idealist—little by little, you've learned to value the love you're able to bestow.

MARCH 9

Extremely smart and articulate, you quickly grasp what's needed to fix a situation. The problem is you want to please, which slows down your decisiveness. You're loving and caring, and too often allow a relationship to be lopsided—with you doing the giving.

MARCH 10

You're a philosopher and artist rolled up in a street-smart, people-charming personality. You're buoyant and entertaining and have wicked humor. You can be dangerous romantically because you're a heartbreaker, but one perfect soulmate is destined to complete you.

MARCH 11

You're a fixed point for others—yet in your own life, you're a wanderer on an indefinable quest. In time, you will be defined by your unusual work. As for love, you find it hard to fulfill your complicated needs, but here, too, you'll end up with someone who adores you.

MARCH 12

In you, elegant style mixes with mischievousness, which magnetizes people. In your work, you come up with clear answers to complex problems, a quality that can make you money. Romantically, you have a flirtatious manner, but this hides a totally faithful heart.

MARCH 13

You are beautiful inside and out, but hard to get to know. You're picky about people and put up shields. Drawn to the arts, you possess unique talent. You have deep emotional strength but also a restless heart—finding perfect love will take you on a complicated journey.

MARCH 14

You have a rebel quality—you're inventive, original, and passionate, and you don't do what's expected. Your strength is your dedication; you'll succeed in one-of-a-kind work. Love brings out your deep capacity for caring, and you must be careful to whom you give yourself.

MARCH 15

You're self-protective, very independent, and a pioneer. You're not interested in work that's been done before. You have a talent for performing and seizing attention. In love, you want to create a safe haven, but it takes a special lover to understand you emotionally.

MARCH 16

You're curious, love ideas, and have an uncanny knack for zeroing in on people who become your ardent fans. Sometimes you spend too long thinking instead of doing. In love, you're dramatic and intense and need to be treated elegantly. You're a passionate and loyal lover.

MARCH 17

Courage sets you apart—you've always faced "what is," and the middle cycle of your life brings great reward. You need to be less hard on yourself, for you're truly gifted. In love, you have powerful desires and a deep capacity to support and cherish.

MARCH 18

You have heroic strength of character, and one day you'll believe this. You're also a bit unworldly and have an arresting glamour. In emotional affairs, you trustingly follow your heart—but you're learning that your first intuitions about a lover are what you should listen to.

MARCH 19

With your powerful mind you can rationalize away feelings, so you're always trying to balance what you feel with what you think.

People see you as an enigma—secretive yet open, intense yet detached—but the one who loves you truly will know how profoundly caring you are.

MARCH 20

Beneath your pleasant exterior, deep fires of passion burn. You're an individualist destined to rule your own creative "kingdom." In love, you must journey through disappointment, but you do know your own heart and will find your way to the lover who completes you.

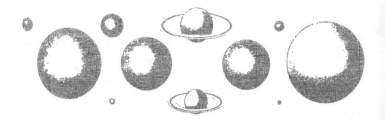

YOU AND CHINESE ASTROLOGY

With Marco Polo's adventurous travels in A.D. 1275, Europeans learned for the first time of the great beauty, wealth, history, and romance of China. Untouched as they were by outside influences, the Chinese developed their astrology along different lines from other ancient cultures, such as the Egyptians, Babylonians, and Greeks in whom Western astrology has its roots. Therefore, the Chinese zodiac differs from the zodiac of the West. To begin with, it is based on a lunar cycle rather than Western astrology's solar cycle. The Chinese zodiac is divided into twelve years, and each year is represented by a different animal—the rat, ox, tiger, rabbit, dragon, snake, horse, goat, monkey, rooster, dog, and pig. The legend of the twelve animals is that when Buddha lay on his deathbed, he asked the animals of the forest to come and bid him farewell. These twelve were the first to arrive. The cat, as the story goes, is not among the animals because it was napping and couldn't be bothered to make the journey. (In some Asian countries, however, such as Vietnam, the cat replaces the rabbit.)

Like Western astrology in which the zodiac signs have different characteristics, each of the twelve Chinese animal years assigns character traits specific to a person born in that year. For example, the Year of the Rat confers honesty and an analytical mind, whereas the Year of the Monkey grants charm and quick ability to take advantage.

Here are descriptions for Pisces for each Chinese animal year:

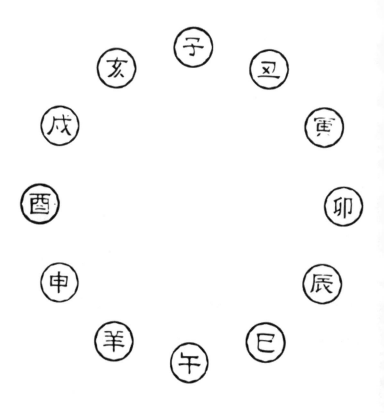

Years of the Rat

1900	1960	2020	2080
1912	1972	2032	2092
1924	1984	2044	
1936	1996	2056	
1948	2008	2068	

The Asian Rat is charming, sprightly, amusing, and highly intelligent. Rat quickness of mind combines with your enticing Piscean allure, creating a captivating personality with infectious wit who can cultivate friends in high places and glean useful information. Rat Years always bring new prospects, especially financial ones, and as a Pisces Rat, you're somewhat of a wizard. Some might say you're an opportunist, but your intentions are high-minded and you're a hard worker who doesn't compromise. It's because you're upbeat and socially beguiling that you're often favored over those with dreary dispositions. You're fun—knowledgeable about the latest fads and fashions, and you love to gossip. Among your sterling qualities is your putting the happiness of those you love over yours. Romantically, you're sentimental and flirtatious, but utterly devoted. Compatible partners are born in the Years of the Monkey, Pig, Rat, and Snake.

IF YOU ARE PISCES BORN IN THE YEAR OF THE OX

Years of the Ox

1901	1961	2021	2081
1913	1973	2033	2093
1925	1985	2045	
1937	1997	2057	
1949	2009	2069	

The Western ox is thought of as plodding and dull, but in Asia the Ox is eloquent, courteous, and sharply intelligent, and inspires confidence. The Ox has strength of purpose, which adds great potency to your Piscean originality. You have excellent taste and impress others with both your in-born antennae about what is really worthy and your work ethic. You're more grounded and stable than many Pisceans. Especially, you have moral courage; a touch of the saint resides in you—and, in some cases, the fanatic. You can be very driven, and you can run into difficulties because of stubborn thinking (e.g., taking a path you're positive will lead to success and closing your mind to anything else). In love, you're emotional and sexual, deeply invested in the other person, and have a penchant for secret relationships. But in marriage, you're committed. Compatible partners are born in the Years of the Rabbit, Rooster, Monkey, Pig, and Snake.

IF YOU ARE PISCES BORN IN THE YEAR OF THE TIGER

Years of the Tiger

1902	1962	2022	2082
1914	1974	2034	2094
1926	1986	2046	
1938	1998	2058	
1950	2010	2070	

The Chinese Tiger is a creature of courage, power, nobility, and magnificence. In ancient China, the Tiger was one of the insignias of the emperor, and to Buddhists it represents faith. To be born a Tiger endows you with beauty and boldness; it's said that luck is your lifelong friend. In you, Tiger fervor and impetuosity combine with Piscean imagination and awareness of others' feelings, giving you radiant magnetism. People are drawn to your energy and compassion, and your belief that things will miraculously turn out well. You have special creative vision and tend to be more daring than many Pisceans. It's true you can get spoiled by attention, and you're also a bit of a rebel—but you're able to carve out your own territory. In love, you're very passionate and your relationships are dramatic. Your heart is tender, though, and you're a sentimental pussycat. Compatible partners are born in the Years of the Rabbit, Dog, Dragon, Monkey, Tiger, and Pig.

Years of the Rabbit

1903	1963	2023	2083
1915	1975	2035	2095
1927	1987	2047	
1939	1999	2059	
1951	2011	2071	

The Asian Rabbit (or, in countries such as Vietnam, the Cat) is loved for its refinement, grace, and glamorous allure. The Rabbit is talkative, theatrical, and richly imaginative. Rabbit cleverness and sociability blend beautifully with Piscean artistic flair; you're gifted in communications and in charming the public. You may think you're a private person, but you were born to be onstage. As a Pisces Rabbit, you have a fun-loving, frivolous side, and in spite of your Piscean bent toward deep thinking, a part of you just wants to have fun. Still, you're powerful when focused on a goal and, in your work, are blessed with farsightedness. You're good at finances even though money interests you just a bit less than expressing yourself. Love and sex are great pleasures, and you're abundantly giving to a lover. You do need to be adored, though, or you may stray. Compatible partners are born in the Years of the Goat, Dog, Dragon, Snake, Horse, and Monkey.

IF YOU ARE PISCES BORN IN THE YEAR OF THE DRAGON

Years of the Dragon

1904	1964	2024	2084
1916	1976	2036	2096
1928	1988	2048	
1940	2000	2060	
1952	2012	2072	

The Asian Dragon is a magnificent being, venerated for its sovereignty and spirituality. In both China and Japan, the Dragon symbolized the emperor, and in Taoist religion it represents the spirit of change. The Dragon confers perseverance and fearlessness that merge with your Pisces creativity, making you inventive and enterprising. Unlike Pisceans who hang back, you'll push into a new venture and give it a try. Inwardly, you may retain your Pisces reticence, but you have Dragon pride and won't let others think less of you. You're very talented and need to feel you're utilizing your splendid gifts. Pisces likes to draw apart from the crowd, and as a Pisces Dragon this shows up as insistence on working independently. With an audience, you have powerful charisma. Romantically, you're seductive and extremely sensual—you do all you can to make an affair a grand passion. Compatible partners are born in the Years of the Rabbit, Goat, Monkey, Snake, and Tiger.

IF YOU ARE PISCES BORN IN THE YEAR OF THE SNAKE

Years of the Snake

1905	1965	2025	2085
1917	1977	2037	2097
1929	1989	2049	
1941	2001	2061	
1953	2013	2073	

The Western snake connotes danger and deceit, but the Asian Snake is a thing of beauty, linked to the Goddess of Beauty and the Sea. The Snake is intuitive, captivating, and mysterious. Snake artistry and acute intelligence magnify your Piscean elegance and fluency of speech, and especially your imaginative powers. You're known for brilliant insights and the wise advice you generously give. The Snake represents renewal, and as a Pisces Snake you have a magical sense of possibility. You're also independent and likely to slither off when people bore you or try to control you. Some say you're cunning and a bit devious, but it's only that your clairvoyant sixth sense immediately spots advantage. You are, in fact, extremely honest and devoted, and when you love someone, you love forever. You also have a decidedly possessive streak. Compatible partners are born in the Years of the Rabbit, Rooster, Dragon, Horse, Ox, and Rat.

IF YOU ARE PISCES BORN IN THE YEAR OF THE HORSE

Years of the Horse

1906	1966	2026	2086
1918	1978	2038	2098
1930	1990	2050	
1942	2002	2062	
1954	2014	2074	

In Asia, the Horse is so powerful that pregnancies are planned around a Horse year. The Horse symbolizes nobility, ambition, and strong individuality—and you, born in a Horse year, will always feel different from others. Horse spiritedness and independence intertwine with your Piscean charisma, and you radiate a special vividness and vibrancy people remember. You have a bohemian quality that belies a dedication to your friendships, work, and commitments. You're multitalented, making it difficult to fix on one thing; you're destined to wander both geographically and emotionally. Happily, you'll find great fulfillment creatively and in relationships. Certainly love is a major "resting place," though not at all serene. You're exuberant, passionate, capable of boundless devotion, and you need someone you can idolize. Compatible partners are born in the Years of the Rabbit, Rooster, Goat, Horse, and Snake.

IF YOU ARE PISCES BORN IN THE YEAR OF THE GOAT

Years of the Goat

1907	1967	2027	2087
1919	1979	2039	2099
1931	1991	2051	
1943	2003	2063	
1955	2015	2075	

The Chinese Goat is engaging and communicative, and has a way of finding fertile fields to thrive in. The Year of the Goat ushers in peace and prosperity, and this is what the Goat tries to create in its life. Goat resourcefulness and ability to charm all types of people underscore your Piscean warmth and fanciful imagination. You are convivial, idealistic, and strongly artistic. You have a love of craft, and whether you're building, performing, putting together a deal, or writing a novel, you give precise attention to detail. People are drawn to your sweet nature and serenity—but beneath your apparent calmness, you churn with emotional energy. Pisces Goat is deeply feeling. Often, because you want to please, you overextend yourself and need to retreat to figure out what *you* want. You're a passionate lover, and your heart yearns for lasting love. After some early stops and starts, you'll find a life mate with whom you can express your pent-up feelings. Compatible partners are born in the Years of the Rabbit, Dragon, Horse, Monkey, and Pig.

IF YOU ARE PISCES BORN IN THE YEAR OF
THE MONKEY

⊕

Years of the Monkey

1908	1968	2028	2088
1920	1980	2040	2100
1932	1992	2052	
1944	2004	2064	
1956	2016	2076	

In Asian mythology, the amusing Monkey is the beloved companion of the God of Sailors, keeping him entertained on long sea voyages. The Monkey is vivacious, witty, irrepressible, and divinely discontent. The Monkey loves change and excitement, which not only adds sparkle to your Piscean imagination, it magnifies your penchant for swimming off in new directions. With your curiosity and rare artistic gifts, you will do original work. You're a generous friend, have a bawdy sense of humor, are sensual and seductive, and have a touch of class in your taste and style. Paradoxes exist: You crave love and attention but are independent; you dote on those you care for but can be mischievous and undependable. You're always on a quest to find more—more experiences, more love, more adventure. Your love affairs are epic and tumultuous, and it's hard to settle down. Compatible partners are born in the Years of the Rabbit, Dragon, Ox, Pig, Rat, and Tiger.

IF YOU ARE PISCES BORN IN THE YEAR OF
THE ROOSTER

Years of the Rooster

1909	1957	2005	2053
1921	1969	2017	2065
1933	1981	2029	2077
1945	1993	2041	2089

Courage is the Rooster's middle name—and in Asia, he is dedicated to the Goddess of the Sun, whom he rescued. The Rooster is honorable, brilliant, outspoken, and sincere. The high goals of the Rooster raise the level of your Piscean creative output, and you are a dreamer who can be assertive about putting your dreams into action. If faced with obstacles, you turn in another direction; you're both determined and resilient. People are enchanted with the way you make each day seem uniquely filled with possibility. You can be a bit of an eccentric (dressing differently or doing unusual work), and your great personal warmth has a certain bite, for you're sharply observant and speak your mind. In love, you're faithful and constant, yet here, too, you make unusual choices (e.g., someone from another culture, someone not free to marry). But you will be happy in love. Compatible partners are born in the Years of the Horse, Ox, and Snake.

Years of the Dog

1910	1958	2006	2054
1922	1970	2018	2066
1934	1982	2030	2078
1946	1994	2042	2090

As in real life, the Asian Dog is the epitome of fidelity and loyal service. The Dog is trustworthy, diligent, and practical, and thus able to care for and accomplish. Dog constancy and guardianship add toughness to your Piscean need to be needed. You show your commitment in work that makes a concrete difference. You can be a firebrand and fighter against what is imbalanced or unjust or will just plain function better; you're a spokesperson and fixer. In relationships, you also take the role of rescuer and the one who looks out for what can go wrong. You're an anxious worrier, and when you're in a down mood you snap and bark. You are, however, deeply sensitive and eager to prove your worth—to be of service. Especially in love, you're fiercely devoted and passionate. Needless to say, you are faithful, though you can be quite possessive. Compatible partners are born in the Years of the Cat, Dog, Pig, and Tiger.

IF YOU ARE PISCES BORN IN THE YEAR OF THE PIG ♓

Years of the Pig

1911	1959	2007	2055
1923	1971	2019	2067
1935	1983	2031	2079
1947	1995	2043	2091

Unlike the lowly Western pig, the Asian Pig is gallant, chivalrous, and cultured—loved for its warmth and honesty. Pig scrupulousness and intellectual brilliance energize your one-of-a-kind Piscean talents, and you're an ambitious accomplisher. You're drawn to the past (e.g., antiques, history, literature, museum work) and known for work that will last. As a Pisces Pig, you also have an instinct for where the money is and at some point will be well-off financially. It's true you can be pigheaded about your ideas, but these are usually nonmainstream and you work independently, so you don't get into too much conflict. Your need for security shows up in relationships. In love especially, you hold fast. You require tons of affection and tenderness; otherwise your soul shrivels up. And you give all your sensuality and deep devotion to your chosen mate. Compatible partners are born in the Years of the Rabbit, Dog, Pig, Ox, and Tiger.

YOU AND NUMEROLOGY

Numerology is the language of numbers. It is the belief that there is a correlation between numbers and living things, ideas, and concepts. Certainly, numbers surround and infuse our lives (e.g., twenty-four hours in a day, twelve months of the year, etc.). And from ancient times, mystics have taught that numbers carry a *vibration*, a deeper meaning that defines how each of us fits into the universe. According to numerology, you are born with a personal number that contains information about who you are and what you need to be happy. This number expresses what numerology calls your life path.

All numbers reduce to one of nine digits, numbers 1 through 9. Your personal number is based on your date of birth. To calculate your number, write your birth date in numerals. As an example, the birth date of February 29, 1978, is written 2-29-1978. Now begin the addition: $2 + 29 + 1 + 9 + 7 + 8 = 56$; 56 reduces to $5 + 6 = 11$; 11 reduces to $1 + 1 = 2$. The personal number for someone born February 29, 1979, is *Two*.

IF YOU ARE A PISCES ONE

Keywords: Confidence and Creativity

One is the number of leadership and new beginnings. You rush into whatever engages your heart—whether a new plan, a love affair, or an adventurous trip. Being a One accentuates your Pisces restlessness but also gives you courage to say yes to adventure. You're able to find unusual, inventive outlets for your creativity, and your work is one of a kind. You can't bear to be under the thumb of other people. Your best careers are those in which you work independently. As for love, you want ecstasy and passion and can be a roses-and-champagne romantic. In lovemaking, you adore playing out your fantasies, and the most exciting part of an affair is the beginning.

IF YOU ARE A PISCES TWO

Keywords: Cooperation and Balance

Two is the number of cooperation and creating a secure entity. Being a Two gives you extra Pisces magnetism—you attract what you need. Your magic is not only your charming people skills but your ability to breathe life into empty forms (e.g., a creative concept, a new relationship) and produce something of worth. You try to draw to you relationships and financial stability so that you're part of a secure "family." In love, you look for a partnership with someone you can trust and share confidences with. You're deeply sensual and understand that the secret to satisfying a lover is to abandon *yourself* to pleasure.

IF YOU ARE A PISCES THREE

Keywords: Expression and Sensitivity

Three symbolizes self-expression. You have a joyful personality. Being a Three magnifies your Pisces gift for words and talent for seeing possibilities. You link people together so that they benefit from each other; you stimulate others to think. Creativity and innovation are your specialties. However, you're easily distracted, seized by enthusiasms that fade as the next new thing arrives. In love, you need someone who excites you intellectually and sensually, and understands your complex personality. Sexually, you're quick tinder—sex is very important in a relationship, though at your core you long for true commitment with a soulmate.

IF YOU ARE A PISCES FOUR

Keywords: Stability and Process

Four is the number of dedication and loyalty. It represents *foundation*, exactly as a four-sided square does. You like to build—especially build a secure life and find peace and contentment. You look for self-expression in your work and loyalty in your relationships. Like most Pisceans, you're filled with imaginative ideas, but you're the one who can take these to a new level. You have persistence. In romance, you adore passionate closeness, and your style of loving is to invest yourself wholly. Sexually, you're an imaginative and generous lover, and you need a giving and understanding partner with whom you can express your rich sensuality.

IF YOU ARE A PISCES FIVE

Keywords: Freedom and Discipline

Five is the number of change and freedom. You're a gregarious nonconformist. You need to perform, to communicate. With your chameleon intellect (it can go in any direction) and captivating ability to deal with people, you charm and influence others. You have potent chemistry with the public. In friendships, you're quick to jump in to give advice and whatever the other needs. Your desire in life is to push past boundaries and express your free spirit. This is true sexually as well, and you are a most inventive lover. But when you give your heart away for keeps, it's to someone with whom you passionately mesh—body and mind.

IF YOU ARE A PISCES SIX

Keywords: Vision and Acceptance

Six is the number of teaching, healing, and utilizing your talents. You're geared toward changing the world, or at least fixing other people's lives. Being an advice giver and even a therapist to your friends comes naturally. Being a Six magnifies your Piscean gift for caring; and you have a way of uplifting others' spirits. Work centers you, and you bring an artisan's eye to everything you do. You tend to be too critical of yourself, though, which can prevent you from aiming for the biggest gains. In love, you're fervent about being a helpmate and confidante—in every respect, you're a true partner. You're also a secret sensualist who opens completely to the one you trust.

IF YOU ARE A PISCES SEVEN

Keywords: Trust and Openness

Seven is the number of the mystic and the intensely focused specialist. You're an intriguing "inner workings" person—you see deeply into human nature, and in a flash understand how things work (in business, between people, etc.). You're an intellectual, a philosopher, and a connoisseur of everything creative. Your heart's desire is to surround yourself with things of value—a loving mate, family, creative work, authentic relationships. At your core, you're extremely loyal and intensely loving, though very selective about relationships. Within you are deep wells of passion, and in love, you need a partner who will stay by your side on your life's journey.

IF YOU ARE A PISCES EIGHT

Keywords: Abundance and Power

Eight is the number of mastery. With your Pisces intelligence and alertness to others, you're able to create opportunities. It's important to you to prove yourself, to do well in your *own* eyes—and since you're exceedingly talented, people and situations open to you. You have both imagination and an analytical mind (a rare combination), and you are seen as an artist at what you do. Your best trait is your total faith to your word; giving your promise in love is a serious act. You're a protective and caring lover and, in turn, must know your lover is your loyal ally. Your deep need is to create a stable base with someone you adore and respect.

Keywords: Integrity and Wisdom

Nine is the path of the "old soul," the number of completion and full bloom. Because it's the last number, it sums up the highs and lows of human experience, and you live a life of dramatic events. You're deeply feeling, extremely protective, interested in all kinds of exploration. You do highly original work, and are an inspiration to others. People see you as colorful and heroic because you have an adventurous outlook but are also spiritual and altruistic. In love, you're truthful and sincere—and also a romantic, sensual creature. As a Pisces Nine, you generously give of yourself, often to the point of sacrificing.

LAST WORD: YOUR PISCES UNFINISHED BUSINESS

Psychologists often use the phrase *unfinished business* to describe unresolved issues—for example, patterns from childhood that cause unhappiness, anger that keeps one stuck, scenarios of family dysfunction that repeat through second and third generations (such as alcoholism or abusive behavior).

Astrology teaches that the past is indeed very much with us in the present. And that using astrological insights can help us move out of emotional darkness into greater clarity. Even within this book (which is not a tome of hundreds of pages) you have read of many of the superlatives and challenges of being Pisces. You have breathtaking gifts and at the same time certain tendencies that can undermine utilizing these abilities.

In nature, a fascinating fact is that in jungles and forests a poisonous plant will grow in a certain spot and always, just a few feet away, is a plant that is the antidote to that specific poison. Likewise, in astrology, the antidote is right there ready to be used when the negatives threaten to overwhelm your life.

At the root of Pisces's unfinished business is the constant pull toward escapism. The desire to escape is a powerful inclination in the Piscean personality, and it takes many forms—among them self-deception, delusional thinking, far-fetched fantasy, denial of situations Pisces doesn't want to deal with, addictive relationships, and reliance on mind-altering substances (such as alcohol and drugs). The ancients called Pisces the sign of Sorrow from Self-Undoing, and you will always suffer misery and bondage when you fail to rise above negative behavior.

In classical astrology, Pisces was associated with confinement (hospitals, prisons, mental institutions, monasteries—places of being shut away or withdrawing into). The Pisces connection to drawing apart is seen in your introspective nature. Psychologically, your tendency is to pull away and withdraw. Whether you go into yourself, your own thoughts and imaginings, your creativity, or whatever you retreat to, you easily absent yourself. Especially, you draw into your fears. And all of Pisces's self-undoing emanates from fear.

Each of the Water signs (Cancer, Scorpio, Pisces) has deep issues surrounding fear. The Water signs are emotional (Water symbolizes emotion), and each struggles with overwhelming emotions. Cancer fears being unsafe, unprotected, and at risk. Scorpio fears loss of control and the resulting chaos. Pisces fears being alone and vulnerable.

Your Piscean fears exhibit themselves in feeling inadequate. You may flee from responsibility because you think you won't measure up. You may turn down a promotion, not submit your creative work for review. Your imagination can run riot with rejection and worst-case scenarios. You may stay in a dysfunctional relationship because you're afraid of what will happen to you if you leave. Too afraid to say no, you give yourself over to martyrdom for others' needs. Many Pisceans allow fear to dictate their choices and are in continual struggle to escape the pain of their terrors.

Yet you possess every tool you need to reverse the Piscean downward spiral. The antidotes are there to be found in their entirety in being Pisces, for you are the sign of spiritual strength. This does not mean religiosity. It means having an almost divine ability to rise above limitations of every kind—personal demons, heartache and disappointment, opportunities denied to you, and even what other people call "real facts." Others see what is, but you see possibilities. You're a dreamer but also a doer, able to approach the most daunting ventures in a state of high expectancy.

Pisces is plugged into a source of inspiration that can be called a higher power. You believe in miracles and will work hard to make them happen. You have extraordinary wisdom; you were born "knowing" things. When it comes to understanding people, no one has your insight and intuition. Pisces is the sign of artistry and imagination, and you are a creative genius capable of concentrated effort. You have the guts to survive and the gift of passion. Among your most precious contributions to this world is your ability to show others how to help themselves.

The day you face yourself in all your glory, and all your frailty, is the day you begin to transform into all you can become. Only the strong are given your treasures. You are far stronger than you can even imagine.

FAMOUS PEOPLE WITH THE SUN IN PISCES

Edward Albee
Mario Andretti
W. H. Auden
Tammy Faye Bakker
Drew Barrymore
Harry Belafonte
Alexander Graham Bell
Osama bin Laden
Erma Bombeck
Elizabeth Barrett Browning
Luther Burbank
Michael Caine
Karen Carpenter
Enrico Caruso
Johnny Cash
Edgar Cayce
Cyd Charisse
Frederic Chopin
Glenn Close
Kurt Cobain
Roy Cohn
Nat King Cole
Nicolaus Copernicus
Tom Courtenay
Cindy Crawford
Billy Crystal
Honore Daumier
Michael Dell
Jimmy Dorsey
Lawrence Durrell
Wyatt Earp
Albert Einstein
Bobby Fischer
Peter Fonda
Galileo Galilei
Ruth Bader Ginsburg
Jackie Gleason
Mikhail Gorbachev
Kelsey Grammer
Cedric Hardwicke
Jean Harlow

George Harrison
Rex Harrison
Patricia Hearst
Ben Hecht
Jennifer Love Hewitt
Winslow Homer
Ron Howard
Victor Hugo
William Hurt
Henrik Ibsen
John Irving
Steve Jobs
Jennifer Jones
Barbara Jordan
Jon Bon Jovi
Kiri Te Kanawa
Edward M. Kennedy
Jack Kerouac
Ring Lardner
Spike Lee
Sybil Leek
Jerry Lewis
Rob Lowe
James Madison
Anna Magnani
Gabriel García Marquez
Michelangelo
Edna St. Vincent Millay
Glenn Miller
Liza Minnelli
Piet Mondrian
Zero Mostel
Rupert Murdoch
Ralph Nader
Kate Nelligan
Vaslav Nijinsky
David Niven
Pat Nixon
Rudolph Nureyev
Merle Oberon
Shaquille O'Neal

Sidney Poitier
Aidan Quinn
Tony Randall
Sally Jessy Raphael
Lynn Redgrave
Carl Reiner
Rob Reiner
Pierre-Auguste Renoir
Miranda Richardson
Bobby Riggs
Nicolai Rimsky-Korsakov
Philip Roth
Kurt Russell
Willard Scott
Neil Sedaka
Dr. Seuss
Irwin Shaw
Dinah Shore
John Steinbeck
Dean Stockwell
Sharon Stone
Darryl Strawberry
Jimmy Swaggart
Elizabeth Taylor
James Taylor
Ellen Terry
Franchot Tone
Tommy Tune
Carrie Underwood
John Updike
Gloria Vanderbilt
Irving Wallace
Earl Warren
George Washington
Kurt Weill
Lawrence Welk
Vanessa Williams
Bruce Willis
Joanne Woodward

PART TWO

ALL ABOUT YOUR SIGN OF PISCES

PISCES'S ASTROLOGICAL AFFINITIES, LINKS, AND LORE

SYMBOL: Two Fishes Tied to One Another and Swimming in Opposite Directions ⮀

Signifying hidden depths, shifting emotional currents, conflicting desires, and extremes of temperament. The two fishes are also said to represent the pull between the material world and the spiritual, as well as opposing energies of male and female.

RULING PLANET: Neptune ♆

The Roman god of the water and the sea. In mythology, Neptune was the brother of Jupiter and Pluto, and each of the three brothers ruled over one kingdom of the universe (Neptune ruled the seas, Jupiter the earth and heavens, and Pluto the underworld). In astronomy, Neptune is the eighth planet from the Sun in our solar system and the second of the "modern" planets to be discovered (in 1846).

Astrologically, Neptune is the planet of illusion, glamour, mystery, and spirituality. Its power is that of fantasy and the imagination. Neptune also holds sway over the subconscious world, escapism, and deception.

DOMINANT KEYWORD

I BELIEVE

GLYPH (Written Symbol))(

The pictograph represents two fishes tied together, each trying to swim in an opposite direction. The curving line that represents a fish was the ancient Egyptian symbol for "fish." The glyph is also a picture of the human feet, the part of the anatomy that Pisces rules. In symbolic terms, the glyph is two crescent moons connected by a straight line. This represents emotion and higher consciousness tied to and limited by the material world.

PART OF THE BODY RULED BY PISCES: The Feet

Pisceans have beautifully shaped, sensitive feet that are unfortunately prone to aches, bunions, corns. Ill-fitting shoes are a particular hazard to people of this sign.

LUCKY DAY: Friday

Friday comes from the Old English *frigedaeg* (Day of Frige), a translation from the Latin for Day of Venus. Venus is planet of love, beauty and the arts, warmth and seduction. Although Pisces's ruling planet is Neptune, Neptune was not discovered until 1846, long after the days of the week had been named. Being the sign of an affectionate nature and deep creativity, Pisces was associated by the ancients with Venus's day of Friday.

LUCKY NUMBERS: 2 and 6

Numerologically, 2 is the number of sensitivity, artistry, insight, and inner wisdom—and 6 is linked to nurturing relationships and the balance of opposites. These qualities align with the nature of Pisces.

TAROT CARD: The Moon

The card in the Tarot linked to Pisces is the Moon. An ancient name for this card is Child of the Sons of the Mighty. In the Tarot, this card signifies the unconscious, intuition, the invisible, and things hidden. It represents nighttime and darkness, and speaks of a transitional period in which to turn inward and wait. The Moon tells you to face your fears and allow your inner knowing to come to the answer. When this card turns up in a reading, it says you are standing in the dark and the outcome is not in your hands. But you will arrive at your goal when the time is right, and triumphing over your uncertainties will be empowering.

The card itself pictures a dog and a wolf baying at the Moon. Dewdrops are falling from the Moon, a pool of water is in the foreground, and a path leads toward the horizon. The Moon symbolizes emotions of fear and anxiety, the pool of water is the unconscious, and the dewdrops are knowledge. The wolf represents untamed desires, the dog is adaptation, and the path to the horizon is a person's spiritual journey.

For Pisces, the Moon tells you to have faith in your inner voice—for by being true to your values, you will stay on the path of enlightenment and always be protected. Be patient, go through the "night," and the light of dawn will come.

MAGICAL BIRTHSTONE: Aquamarine

A gemstone prized for its sublime blue-green color and its use as a talisman. The name *aquamarine* comes from the Latin *aqua marina*, meaning "water of the sea." This stone was sacred to many of the sea deities, linked to sea goddesses and mermaids, and connected to the concept of the Mother Goddess (the Great Mother). Ancient sailors believed the aquamarine would give them safe passage across the oceans and protection against storms at sea. Roman fishermen carried the stone to help ensure a bountiful catch. The gemstone was also believed to be an antidote for poison. For Pisceans, the aquamarine brings serenity of mind, magnifies occult powers, and protects while traveling on the sea.

SPECIAL COLORS: Pale Green and Turquoise

The dreamy colors of the sea. Pale green symbolizes hope, new life, and fertility, and turquoise is the color of calmness and serenity.

CONSTELLATION OF PISCES

Pisces is the Latin plural for "fish." The Greeks and Persians both called this constellation "Fish," and to the Babylonians it was "Two Tails." The Babylonian image was two fish swimming in two converging streams of water, which was a basic map of the land of Mesopotamia set between the Tigris and Euphrates rivers. According to one Greek myth, the constellation of Pisces represented Aphrodite and her son Eros, who were transformed into two fishes in order to escape from the monster Typhon. They were tied together to ensure they would never lose one another.

CITIES

Casablanca, Alexandria, Lisbon, Seville, Dublin

COUNTRIES

Portugal, the Sahara Desert

FLOWERS

Water Lily, White Poppy, and Jonquil

TREES

Fig and Willow

HERBS AND SPICES

Chicory, Lime, and Mosses

METAL: Platinum

A lustrous, silvery-white precious metal used in fine jewelry and industrially. Because of its rarity, platinum carries an association with wealth and prestige. Platinum was highly prized in pre-Columbian Central and South America, and then discovered by the Spanish conqistadors. In Spain it became widely used by royalty and the wealthy for their artifacts, art, heraldry, and jewelry; the late 1700s in Spain is known as the Platimum Age.

On an esoteric level, the qualities of platinum—its value, purity, preciousness, and unusual beauty—align with Piscean sensitivity, spirituality, inner radiance, and esoteric knowledge.

ANIMALS RULED BY PISCES

Fish, Dolphins, Whales, Porpoises

DANGER

Pisceans have a high susceptibility to alcohol and drugs. They are also easily drawn into unpredictable situations and to unbalanced people.

PERSONAL PROVERBS

Some things have to be believed to be seen.

All is flux. You cannot step twice into the same river.

KEYWORDS FOR PISCES

Imaginative
Receptive
Intuitive
Emotional
Impressionable
Romantic
Subtle
Mysterious
Psychic
Spiritual
Believer in miracles
Devoted
Nurturing
Compassionate

Self-sacrificing
Sentimental
Easily hurt
Humanistic
Passive
Procrastinating
Indirect
Changeable
Gullible
Dependent
Introverted
Unfocused
Escapist
Depressive
Isolationist

HOW ASTROLOGY SLICES AND DICES YOUR SIGN OF PISCES

DUALITY: Feminine

The twelve astrological signs are divided into two groups, *masculine* and *feminine*. Six are masculine and six are feminine; this is known as the sign's *duality*. A masculine sign is direct and energetic. A feminine sign is receptive and magnetic. These attributes were given to the signs about 2,500 years ago. Today modern astrologers avoid the sexism implicit in these distinctions. A masculine sign does not mean "positive and forceful" any more than a feminine sign means "negative and weak." In modern terminology, the masculine signs are defined as outer-directed and strong through action. The feminine signs, such as your sign of Pisces, are self-contained and strong through inner reserves.

TRIPLICITY (ELEMENT): Water

The twelve signs are also divided into groups of three signs each. These three-sign groups are called a *triplicity*, and each of these denotes an *element*. The elements are *Fire*, *Earth*, *Air*, and *Water*. In astrology, an element symbolizes a fundamental characterization of the sign.

The three *Fire* signs are Aries, Leo, and Sagittarius. Fire signs are active and enthusiastic.

The three *Earth* signs are Taurus, Virgo, and Capricorn. Earth signs are practical and stable.

The three *Air* signs are Gemini, Libra, and Aquarius. Air signs are intellectual and communicative.

The three *Water* signs are Cancer, Scorpio, and Pisces. Water signs are emotional and intuitive.

QUADRUPLICITY (QUALITY): Mutable

The twelve signs are also divided into groups of four signs each. These four-sign groups are called a *quadruplicity*, and each of these denotes a *quality*. The qualities are *Cardinal*, *Fixed*, and *Mutable*. In astrology, the quality signifies the sign's interaction with the outside world.

Four signs are *Cardinal** signs. They are Aries, Cancer, Libra, and Capricorn. Cardinal signs are enterprising and outgoing. They are the initiators and leaders.

Four signs are *Fixed*. They are Taurus, Leo, Scorpio, and Aquarius. Fixed signs are stubborn, loyal, willful, and they hold on. They are perfectors and finishers, resistant to pressures from the outside (opinions, rules, etc.).

---

*When the Sun crosses the four cardinal points in the zodiac, we mark the beginning of each of our four seasons. Aries begins spring; Cancer begins summer; Libra begins fall; Capricorn begins winter.

Four signs are *Mutable*. They are Gemini, Virgo, Sagittarius, and Pisces. Mutable signs are flexible, versatile, and adaptable. They are able to adjust to differing circumstances.

Your sign of Pisces is a Feminine, Water, Mutable sign—and no other sign in the zodiac is this exact combination. Your sign is a one-of-a-kind combination, and therefore you express the characteristics of your duality, element, and quality differently from any other sign.

For example, your sign is a *Feminine* sign, meaning you are receptive, captivating, caring, and protective. You're a *Water* sign, meaning you're creative, imaginative, deeply feeling, and intuitive. And you're a *Mutable* sign, meaning you're able to go with the flow, adjust, be of service, and quickly adapt to new people and situations.

Now the sign of Cancer is also Feminine and Water, but unlike Pisces (which is Mutable), Cancer is Cardinal. Like you, Cancer is nurturing and protective, is sensitive to the feelings of others, and uses its creativity in highly imaginative ways. But Cancer is exceedingly driven (often compulsive) in its work and displays force in going after an objective. Cancer is an initiator, not a follower, and can become a self-serving opportunist when it sees an advantage. You, being Mutable, are much more cooperative and flexible. You have patience with people and willingness to bend with changing circumstances. You'll learn a new method, see various points of view. In particular, you have enormous fluidity when it comes to dealing with other people's fluctuating emotions, needs, moods, and whims.

Scorpio, too, is Feminine and Water, but unlike Pisces (which is Mutable), Scorpio is Fixed. Like you, Scorpio is deeply creative and protective, and can see into the hearts of other people. It shares with you the characteristics of being emotional, magnetic, and mysterious. However, being Fixed, Scorpio is controlling, unyielding, dominating, and relentless. It needs to have power over its environment—and its fixity is seen in its tight grip over relationships and work, and in being the "survivor" who outlasts all opposition. Lacking your fluid ability to blend into others, Scorpio can cut itself off from the very emotional support it needs. You, on the other hand, flow with the changing current. You cooperate with whatever is going on—your chameleon quality resonates with the emotional temperature around you. You adapt yourself to an altered situation or another person's feelings and don't enforce strict rules or boundaries.

POLARITY: Virgo

The twelve signs are also divided into groups of two signs each. These two-sign groups are called a *polarity* (meaning "opposite"). Each sign in the zodiac has a polarity, which is its opposite sign in the other half of the zodiac. The two signs express opposite characteristics.

Pisces and Virgo are a polarity. Pisces is the sign of fantasy, imagination, insight, inner life, and spiritual knowledge. You are the imaginative dreamer who can do unusual creative work. With a psychic, intuitive approach to life, you have a sixth sense that helps you understand things in a flash—for example, what someone is thinking or an unexpressed problem. Your special skill is as a healer, for you have empathy when anyone is hurt. You feel things deeply, have compassion, and tend to take on the role of looking after people. You're also a quintessential romantic.

Pisces has been called the sign of the mystic, for you are much in tune with things unseen (dreams, visions, impressions, fantasies, reveries). You are guided by the inspirational—you're likely to step out of the rat race and do your creative thing. You have inner resources on which to draw. Pisces is an idealist who was born with faith—and whether this faith is in a higher being or your own values, it sustains you through the amazing flow of your life, the gamut of the human condition.

Virgo, your opposite sign, shares with you a bent toward serving—but Virgo does this in a utilitarian way. Virgo is the sign of work, usefulness, and perfection; it enters situations with an eye to improving them. With an instinct for spotting flaws, Virgo is the one who tries to make the world run correctly. People rely on Virgo for advice, assistance, and an industrious, can-do attitude. This sign's high intelligence combined with high standards produces a dedicated doer with an efficient, no-nonsense approach.

Among Virgo's many superlative qualities (such as loyalty, dependability, being responsible), perhaps its finest is conscientiousness. The Virgo way is to give its best to every detail—nothing is too small or insignificant. Painstaking thoroughness is a Virgo trademark, and being scrupulously honest defines the Virgo character. Virgo people need to be needed; they find meaning in being of use. And they are very practical in how they structure and organize their work. They don't entertain unrealistic ideas. They also have refined taste and style, so when a Virgo takes hold of a project, others know it will not only be done right but have an elegant perfection. Virgo is able to merge a knowledge of what's appropriate with a dedicated work ethic—and therefore leaves wannabe dilettantes far behind in the dust.

Astrologically, Pisces can benefit from adopting some of Virgo's diligent commitment. Virgo is intent on fulfilling the task and doesn't let itself off the hook. It doesn't have Pisces's escapist tendencies. Pisces may have glorious dreams of what *might be*, but possibility will always remain just that if day-after-day effort is missing. Virgo is fond of saying, "It's easy to be successful; all you have to do is work at it constantly." You, Pisces, can learn a valuable lesson from Virgo's stick-to-it-iveness.

In turn, Virgo has much to learn from you, and at the top of this list is your sense of magic, your open-ended attitude. You refuse to be restricted in your thinking. You believe that if you can imagine it, you can create it. And when you combine your dreams with focused work, you do indeed produce miracles. Pisces wants to do something great with its life, make a lasting contribution. You have the vision, and when you're motivated, you have the persistence.